In memory of
Marion & Ross Woodman
& Fraser Boa

To Infinity and Beyond:

The Power of Animation and its Application to Mental Health & Well-being

Quint Boa & James Earl

Contents

Introduction 7

What is animation? 9

A history of animation 11

Four types of animation 15

The power of animation for communication 19

Animation in corporate environment 23

The theory of animation as an intervention 27

Real-world therapeutic applications 31

Conclusion 33

Introduction

Animation is as old as film. It started with *The Humpty Dumpty Circus* in 1898. While there are apparently no surviving copies (only stills of the opening frame), it is generally believed to be the first use of 'stop-motion' animation.

Subsequent major landmarks in the development of animation include – among thousands of others – *Steamboat Willie* (1928), *Snow White and the Seven Dwarfs* (1937), *Tom & Jerry* (1940), *The Flintstones* (1960), *Jurassic Park* (1993), *Toy Story* (1995) and, more recently, *Frozen* (2013) and the latest Marvel Cinematic Universe blockbusters (2022).

Producing animation was traditionally a labour-intensive, and thus costly, endeavour. However, in recent times, with the development of fast computing (and, in particular, software advances in the last ten years), it has become possible to produce animation much more cheaply.

Even before this dramatic drop in cost, the application of animation to television commercials and for corporate communication was obvious, with businesses clamouring to harness its power. And the clamour has only increased since costs of production have dropped.

But, away from the demands of industry, there are other ways the power of animation can be exploited, in socially useful areas. One of the most interesting applications for animation is around mental health, especially that of young adults.

While we all enjoy animation – feel engaged with it, moved by it – there has been little research into why animation has this power. Using the latest imaging techniques such as MRI, in the so-called 'decade of the brain' (Holmes), we have gained an insight into how animation works on the brain and the psychology behind it. While we're a long way from knowing what turns the water of neurochemicals into the wine of consciousness (Edelman), it's becoming clear our sense of reality, while structured through language, is rooted in our pre-language visual and auditory perception.

This ability to produce high-end animation, combined with the latest therapeutic insights, has applications for psychotherapy. If psychotherapy is 'walking with a client', offering them ways of reinterpreting their experiences, then animation offers a fascinating new modality through which these alternatives can be explored. Given the double-digit rise of mental health problems post-pandemic, animation offers a cost-effective way to address and engage clients.

This short booklet aims to explore the power of animation in general, its history and recent commercial applications. It suggests that animation can be applied as an agile and effective tool during the therapeutic process, both in its own right and as an adjunct to existing psychotherapeutic approaches.

What is animation?

Put simply, animation can be defined as a sequence of still images played at speed to create the illusion of motion. But, of course, animation is literally in the eye of the beholder. In order to understand what animation is, we have to do a bit of biology and understand how the eye works.

In terms of our own childhood, many of us have played with animation by creating a stick man. By drawing in sequence in a paper book and then quickly flipping the pages, the stick man can be seen to walk. The magical number here is 24 frames per second. It's at that speed the maximum fluidity is met.

Why 24 frames per second? Because the human eye has become exquisitely adapted over aeons to look for food and avoid danger. To achieve this, the retina moves around five times per second to look for change. It is the fastest movement in the human body. For reasons still not fully understood, that magic number of 24fps seems the ideal speed to choreograph between the changes in an image and the ability of the human eye to perceive them. The fancy term for this illusion of motion is the stroboscopic effect. What we see is literally a series of split-second, cognitive constructions, subtly melded by our brain.

Of course, the biology of perception is full of 'make-dos'. The eye has two blind spots which are essentially painted over. If you hold out your arm and look at your own thumbnail, that's all you can see in high definition in full colour at once.

Colour, of course, doesn't exist but is imputed from nerve impulses received down the optic nerve. Men and women see the colours red and green differently because men require a slightly longer wavelength than women in order to experience the same hue; the grass really is greener for men than it is for women.

(If you're interested in the statement 'colour doesn't exist', have a look at John Locke's idea of primary and secondary qualities, where the shape of something is primary fact about the object, whereas its colour is secondary, and arises only in our perceptions.)

Meaning is the final part of the menu. Anything we see is instantly given a subjective value, derived from context. What two people actually see may be broadly the same but what they 'see' may be very different. A glass of red wine can instantly mean something very different to different people.

And by 'instantly', we mean before we actually 'see' it. Preconscious 'blindsight' means that a hose might be mistaken for a snake, micro aggressions can be seen in others' expressions, and context cues (an ice cream van, a football rolling in the road, a mum running down the pavement) may warn a driver (as long as they aren't texting, of course).

So although animation is 'just' a series of still images, it packs a huge punch. It's interesting to compare animation to video, which is subtly different and a more literal medium. Video engages the viewer at a cognitive level. It uses context cues and selective attention to create a scene, whereas animation is seductive. As it's not 'real', the audience (especially children) tend to suspend their cognitive engagement, for example prejudice, and are lulled into simply watching. The animator is granted unrestricted emotional access to the audience. The cognitive, rational part of the audience's mind kicks in but only after the animation has finished.

While the biological functioning of the eye has been understood for some time, the most recent work in psychology, neuroscience and psychiatry is finally shedding light on how human perception works. Animation, far from being something that is viewed, is a choreography between the animator and the audience, all played out at 24fps.

Telling stories with pictures is an ancient human activity. For the last one hundred years we have been able, through animation, to tell stories with *moving* pictures. In fact, as we shall see, it may be that animation is a lot older than this. The story of this development is fascinating.

A history of animation

Animation has a rich and interesting history. It's worth a (very) quick tour of this history to understand how we arrived at the four styles of animation we enjoy today. This history shows how animation is weaved into culture and cultural change. It also sets the scene for how animation can be used within the therapeutic process and within 'wellness' departments in organisations.

It's often thought that animation is a relatively new visual medium but, arguably, animation is as ancient as our species; certainly older than our ability to use language to communicate. Cave paintings from 200,000 years ago in Altamira show representations of buffalo handprinted onto the walls, deep within the caves. Some of these animals have multiple legs in different poses. It's been suggested these images would have appeared to move when seen by flickering firelight.

Modern animation started with stop motion at the turn of the last century. The developments within movie production during the 1920s were quickly adopted by animators and led to *Steamboat Willie* (1928) and the 'birth' of Mickey Mouse – the (ahem) poster boy of animation.

To make a feature-length animation was a very labour-intensive, expensive process and studios such as Disney had to employ an assembly line of artists. In pursuit of the most cost-efficient process, Walt Disney developed hand drawn, or 'cel', animation. This was essentially a series of cellophane sheets in multiple layers. The bottom layer was the background (a forest); moving up was the character (Snow White's body); and then you arrived at the foreground (Snow White eating an apple).

Meanwhile, the development of stop-motion animation continued and found huge commercial success when it became blended with film. Good examples are *King Kong* (1933) and Harryhausen's *Jason and the Argonauts* (1963).

The revolutionary new medium of television adopted animation in the 1960s, epitomised by the wonderful Hanna-Barbera productions of *The Flintstones* (1960), *Top Cat* (1961), *Wacky Races* (1968) and *Scooby Doo* (1969). Even earlier, Warner Bros had produced *Looney Tunes* (1930) with Bugs Bunny, Daffy Duck and Road Runner, among others, who also became TV favourites.

It became an American ritual for children to sit for hours on a Saturday morning watching cartoons. (And, frankly, who can blame them?)

In addition to these lovely imports, UK children's television produced classic stop-motion animation in *The Magic Roundabout* (1965) and *The Clangers* (1969).

The next inflection point was the 3D revolution, which relied upon computing power. It premiered with the release of *Jurassic Park* (1993), which still regularly charts as the best movie of all time. Computers revolutionised animation production. When Sam Neill and Laura Dern looked at those diplodocuses, we were all looking at the future of 3D movie production.

Jurassic Park heralded the first fully computer-generated movie, *Toy Story* (1995), by Pixar Animation Studios. The financial success of *Toy Story* ensured it was the forerunner of many of today's computer-generated imagery (CGI) movies: *A Bug's Life* (1998), *Shrek* (2001), *Finding Nemo* (2003) and *Frozen* (2013).

3D animation still sets the bar for commercial success with *Avatar* (2009). *Avatar* developed motion capture, which allowed animation to be mapped onto actors.

Stop motion continued its movie success with *Wallace and Gromit: A Grand Day Out* (1989), which was Aardman Animations' highest-grossing animation until *Chicken Run* (2000). Aardman continues pioneering, blockbuster stop motion to this day.

Animation is set to make perhaps its greatest leap with the virtual world of the so-called 'metaverse'. While the benefits of the metaverse remain an open question, it illustrates how animation has been co-opted as a communications tool. To quote Buzz Lightyear, we really are about to go 'to infinity and beyond'.

Animation has been around, in some form, for as long as we have. The emergence of mass entertainment shows how the power of animation to communicate in creative and engaging ways is unique. Animated characters, such as Mickey Mouse and Bugs Bunny, are still some of the world's biggest brands. Animated motion pictures are also some of the highest-grossing films of all time (*Toy Story* series $3.3bn, *Avatar* $3bn, *Up* $700m, *WALL.E* $500m).

This huge entertainment value of animation speaks to its power to engage and evoke feelings. Before we go on to look at how the world of business co-opted animation, let's look first at the four styles of animation emerging in its history.

Each of the four styles is familiar to us; we see them every day. Each has fallen dramatically in cost to produce. But, from a psychotherapeutic point of view, it's interesting to review how these different styles convey information in subtly different ways; and, of course, how these styles can be applied within the therapeutic process.

Four types of animation

We can say there are (broadly) four types of animation which regularly appear on our screens today, whether those screens are at the cinema or on mobile phones. (Animators around the world might disagree, but this is a helpful basic model of animation styles.)

Of course, these styles can be merged and, in addition, new styles may emerge as technology develops.

We can break animation into 2D and 3D, with a subset of two styles of animation each:

2D Animation

Motion Graphics
This combines motion characters and graphics. Following on from diagrams and infographics, the 2D format evolved to motion graphics. Motion graphics works by using prepared graphic elements, for example, characters, shapes and text. It's the type of animation you'd most frequently see on television. It's the animation style most commonly used for things like explainer videos, for example, industrial supply chains or how a server talks to a cloud. If you're trying to explain how a 'thing' works, motion graphics is probably the go-to.

Traditional (cel) Animation
If you think of *Snow White* (1937), you're thinking cel (celluloid) animation, which has a beautiful hand-drawn effect. As we've seen, Disney

used to have hundreds of animators working on one image at a time but now, thanks to digital technology, digital cel animation has developed. This means it's possible for just one animator / illustrator to create the beautiful hand-drawn effect. Cel animation is mostly used for emotive story-led pieces, sensitive topics or public information campaigns, for example, disability awareness.

3D Animation

CGI

As we've seen, the revolution in computer-generated imagery (CGI) began with *Toy Story* (1995) and continues to this day within, for example, the Marvel Cinematic Universe. The rapid advancements in computer technology have meant commercial applications abound. For instance, it's become relatively easy to import CAD files of, say, a BMW car and manipulate them as a photorealistic digital duplicate within a car commercial.

Stop Motion

Finally, stop-motion animation. We've seen the heritage of stop motion as a medium, and its mass appeal through, for example, *Wallace and Gromit* (1989). The cost of its production has plummeted recently with the use of DSLR cameras and prosumer software such as Dragonframe. One of the main production costs now is the creation of models, which need to be animated.

Although animation styles differ wildly, each speaks to the audience in a subtly different way. What they share is a plummet in the cost of production, which makes animation affordable for use within the profession of psychotherapy.

Mixed media art therapy can be created and produced through stop motion in the style of *Charlie and Lola* (2005). Artistic illustration can be brought to life through cel animation such as Raymond Briggs' *The Snowman* (1982). Cognitive approaches can use motion graphics to explain clients' snags, traps and dilemmas. Character-based animation using 2D or 3D can beautifully illustrate scenarios.

To look more closely at why we might use animation to communicate, we need to look at its unique qualities as a medium. Animation can describe things in a way video cannot, and this ability can be harnessed by psychotherapy.

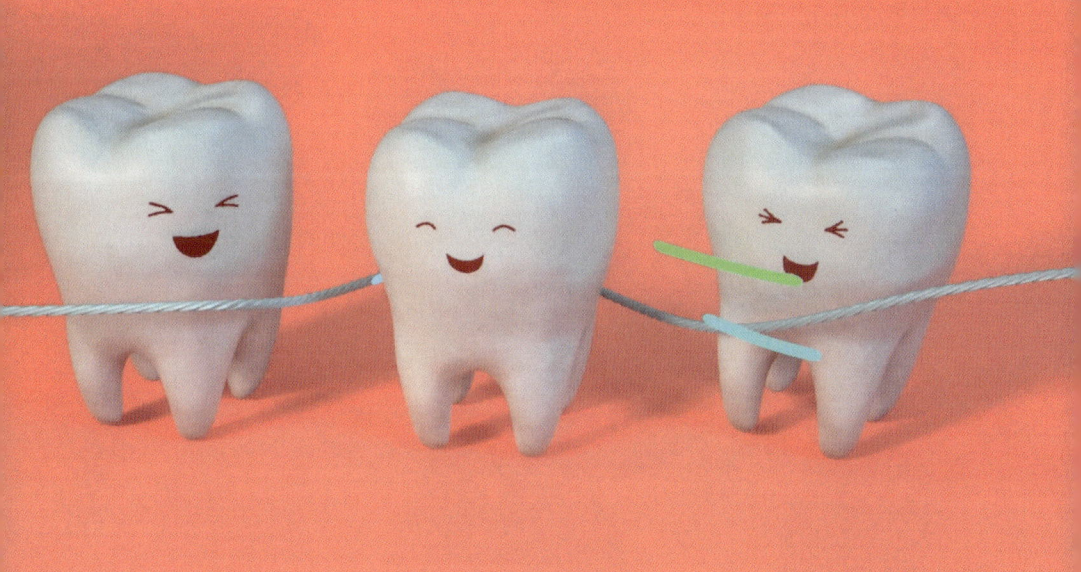

The power of animation for communication

Animation has the power to convey meaning through images in creative and dynamic ways. In particular, animation has an unparalleled ability to describe, interpret and explain. And at times animation is the *only* medium for certain types of subject. These can be summarised as *too big, too small, too complex.*

If a subject is too big to film, you need animation. For example, to show how a planet crashed into the Earth to create the Moon.

If a subject is too small to film, you need animation. For example, to illustrate a microscopic event such as a macrophage attacking a virus.

If a subject is too complex, you need animation. For example, the relationship of dozens of aircraft to air traffic control.

If you want to describe a planet, a microbe, the working of an airport – you'll probably need one of the four types of animation we've described. The exact type will depend on what is trying to be conveyed.

In addition to *too big, too small, too complex*, we can add *too abstract*. Just as language is extended through metaphor, animation goes beyond language because it is inherently a metaphoric medium.

Let's look at animation's power to convey abstract ideas. This potential is probably the most interesting area for psychotherapy.

As Yuval Harai (et al) so eloquently said, humans can't help but create stories. The brain is not just a receptor of sense data, it's a storytelling device. These stories don't just follow sense data (or the rules of physics) – we project stories onto the world and see the world through our stories.

By way of illustration, an oft-repeated child psychology experiment is to show three-year-old children a series of animated shapes, for example, a large blue triangle and some red squares. Depending on how the elements move, the children will offer a variety of themes for the stories they've witnessed, such as the triangle could be 'bullying' or 'playful' with the squares.

Language and thought provide the threads to weave these stories from the world around us. Though these stories feel real, they are only a subjective interpretation, a symbolic re-presentation of the world we inhabit. In a sense we animate, or re-present, our own world as images to ourselves.

In psychotherapy, this is to say we change reality by interpreting it.

If we animate our own world, animation becomes the most powerful way to tell stories and, in so doing, change the world.

Language alone can be a clumsy tool to describe and process the subtleties of feelings to ourselves or others. In particular, the ability of language to communicate as text depends on the reading and writing skills of an audience. For example, a child with ADHD or dyslexia may respond to text in a negative way, while embracing the visual delight of animation. The cognitive 'bandwidth' of a person with depression or experiencing substance withdrawal is such that they may be unable to read a pamphlet.

In fact, language and thought can only take us so far before, like a handrail, we come to rely upon myth, metaphor and symbolism to help us cognitively shuffle along. (This breakdown of language opens us to the realm of poetry; poetry takes the essence of a metaphorical concept and then equates it with a thing. 'Love' becomes 'like a red, red rose'.)

Myth, metaphor and symbolism are where animation reigns supreme. Animation can reimagine the world in a limitless way, enabling us to revisit our earlier appreciation of the world. Like music, animation can be a 'doorway', speaking to us beyond the realm of language and allowing us to briefly suspend the rational, cognitive side of ourselves.

The 'old' view of the mind is that the world is flooding in and we're sitting back just trying to process it all. Our minds are basically passive and reactive, always a step behind. The latest interdisciplinary research shows we don't just react to the world, we anticipate it. Our minds are fundamentally active and predictive. These predictions are largely based upon past experience, our own life stories learnt from childhood. And our predictions aren't idle guesses: they shape how we experience the world. Through symbolic thought and language we live by the scripts we have written, and these scripts determine the quality of our lives, our happiness and wellbeing.

Part of animation's power is that it works to bypass the predictive, rational, cognitive process. Using metaphor, for example, it can subtly model alternate possibilities and this has implications for the therapeutic process. Descriptive imagery can be used to sensorially access areas of the client's mind that were previously closed; to explore and perhaps 'unlock' suppressed thoughts and emotions that they 'couldn't' allow themselves to express even to themselves.

Like fairy tales, animation is powerful in helping to 'understand, constellate and communicate ideas to ourselves' (Bettelheim).

Animation in corporate environment

Having reviewed what animation is, how it developed and its power as a communication tool, it's time to take a quick look at how it's been applied in the world of corporate communications. Since the cost of animation production rapidly fell within corporate budgets, business has embraced it as a cost-effective communication resource. Companies invest heavily in the ability of animation to communicate complex ideas and concepts.

This sheds light on the multiple ways in which psychotherapy can adopt animation as a cost-effective tool within the therapeutic process and, more broadly, within public health information campaigns.

The uptake by businesses was tentative at first. When, in 2012, the latest iterations of the software that was to become the dominant player (Adobe After Effects) were commercially released, computers could begin to create basic animations but lacked the processing and render power to deliver those animations consistently and quickly.

For organisations, simple animations were a 'nice to have' – for example, an animated logo or animated name straps. Animated text and metrics began to be used behind a talking head to add emphasis and highlight key points. And then things exploded.

From 2014 onwards, improvements in technology meant animation became a cost-effective communications tool, both technically and financially. This has led to an exponential growth of its use.

Coupled with these advancements in technology, there was also an increase in the speed of the internet, rapid uptake of smartphone use and, of course, the rise of social media as a direct communication channel between companies and their customers.

Within organisations, 'millennials' with a lifetime of familiarity around tech gradually became decision makers within marketing and comms departments. They advanced the business case for animation to their bosses who commissioned it. The copycat principle meant this initial use of animation by one business rippled quickly out via competitor and challenger companies.

The uptake of animation accelerated to early 2020, and the Covid pandemic increased it still further (when location filming became impossible and the whole world was tethered to its screens). The rollout of Zoom meant it became normal to have full-screen video on a computer screen.

Now animation was possible technically and relatively cheaply, business leveraged the power of animation to communicate.

Obviously the *too big, too small, too complex, too abstract* concepts outlined previously were perfect for the commercial world, especially as this world had itself become harder and harder to explain. After all, the 'fourth industrial revolution' wasn't being driven by anything as picturesque as a printing press, steam locomotive or internal combustion engine. Certain industries such as IT were in the business of producing little black boxes that did amazing things – control thousands of CCTV cameras, move satellites, crunch huge amounts of data, etc – but were definitely not photogenic. How to define the USP of one product from another?

Animation could easily describe and explain the features of how these things worked. If you wanted to 'explode' a tape drive to show its constituent parts, you could. You could also show things invisible to the human eye, like clouds of data or the lethal action of a virus.

As globalisation expanded, companies needed to communicate with thousands of staff, in training and development, in ways which were culturally sensitive. Animation offered that possibility both because it's anonymous and because animation can be easily localised simply by changing the voice-over. The necessity for this business case was reinforced during Covid and the subsequent increase in 'hybrid' work.

Animation has become ubiquitous as a mode of communication in every area of business: internal and external comms, B2B and B2C. The falling cost of animation production, combined with the fact it's practically 'free to air', meant business quickly realised the commercial potential and invested in its production as a communications tool.

The power of animation as a clinical tool resides at the intersection of the latest interdisciplinary research. This sheds light on the ability of animation to describe complex subjects in engaging and relatable ways. Taking a lead from business, those same benefits of animation can be conferred upon many areas of mental health, from individual counselling to national awareness campaigns.

At a time when healthcare budgets are being squeezed, animation offers a strong commercial proposition. It's very quick to produce. It's very flexible, in terms of its ability to be quickly re-edited for different demographics, locations or languages.

And as there's no media space to be bought, animation can be distributed over every platform, channel and format essentially free of charge – it's 'free to air'. As the costs of animation production continue to fall, it becomes a viable modality for the profession of psychotherapy as well.

Animation is also a cheap and dramatically effective medium to address the *too big, too small, too complex, too abstract* concepts in mental well-being.

The theory of animation as an intervention

One of the unique powers of animation is that it can help us access the unconscious.

Used as a mental health tool, therefore, it can be extremely powerful. The ability of animation to reach deep into that repository of symbols, signs and pre-language perceptions we all carry in deep memory is unique to this medium.

Animation can achieve this because the world it shows us is fluid, magical and unconstrained by our knowledge of how things are 'meant' to behave. In an animation, we can fly, teacups can talk and anxiety can be an octopus hugging us.

In our award-winning and most widely viewed two-minute animation on anxiety, for example, we depict anxiety as an octopus, which can both protect us but also restrict us. The visual metaphor often evokes strong emotional reactions from the viewer, and can begin the process of healing.

This visual world is the world we all inhabited before language, one that had no rules and where everything was possible. Before language, there were not even discrete 'things'. The world of 'things' becomes established through language. The baby doesn't know where its own body ends and its mother's body begins, because it has not yet named them as different.

In animation, the thingness of things can be given up again; we can return to that un-boundaried state where bodies merge and everything is pure perception, feeling and desire.

This power of animation to take us back to an earlier state of being has three therapeutic advantages:

1. We are learning at our fastest in that period before we have acquired language. Because animation evokes this early stage of life, it has a huge pedagogic advantage, lulling us out of language and into a feeling state with intense learning potential.

2. It allows the transmission of ideas that are not robbed of their immediate perceptual reality by being constrained by language. So, for example, the cold, grey cloud of depression is no longer a language metaphor but something immediately seen and felt.

3. This 'reaching back' which animation can achieve reconnects us with our own individual unconscious desires, fears and dilemmas. Anxiety, depicted as an octopus, makes you cry or laugh, and makes you feel protective; perhaps for the first time you realise that anxiety was protecting you, and you should protect it.

This reconnection with the unconscious makes animation similar to the world of dream and phantasy, both of which are common tools for psychotherapy. If dreams and phantasy are symbolic representations of our hidden desires, fears and dilemmas, then animation is the perfect medium for both accessing and representing these.

Animation does not show you a flat photographic picture of the world but, more powerfully, a deeply felt experience of it. The octopus of anxiety looks sad when we try to get rid of it. And so our perception of anxiety changes, all without words, without presenting an explicit theory, and yet intensely understood.

The internal world of humans changes when, as young children, we begin to acquire language. Language makes the world a more comprehensible, less magical place, with defined rules and boundaries. While this offers us undoubted safety and control, it also limits our experience. Synaesthesia is the paradigm case of a breakdown in the normal language order: the taste of coffee should not evoke the sound of violins, and sadness cannot be yellow. Yet in the pre-language phase all these rules are moot, just as in a dream. And animation can capture this freedom.

While, to quote Jaques Lacan, 'the unconscious is structured like a language', it is not limited to language. The unconscious uses symbolic forms, like a language, but is free to break the rules of what Michel Foucault calls the order of things.

Animation, likewise, can convey ideas symbolically – in the form of language – but is free to break the rules of the order of things.

In this way, animation frees our imagination and keys into our dream world. Real-life video, on the other hand, is very similar to our language-world interpretation of our surroundings; it is the conscious, compared to animation's unconscious.

Using Freud's formulation of the unconscious, conscious and pre-conscious (that area of our psyche that can be brought into consciousness), we can see how animation can help us bring unconscious material into the pre-conscious. Therapeutic work using animation aims to take this newly conscious material and walk with the client to make it meaningful.

Because we all instinctively recognise animation as taking us back to an earlier iteration of ourselves, we find it inherently soothing – lulling, even – and that state of charmed innocence is the most open to learning. So animation not only gives us symbolic access to our unconscious but puts us into a state to receive it.

A parallel to the power of animation can be found in music. Music is a highly structured symbolic form which expresses meaning but without language. It, too, can lull us into a receptive state in seconds and it, too, has the power to transform our feelings from happy to sad or from sad to uplifted, apparently effortlessly.

In another parallel, music can have lyrics, just as an animation can have a voice-over. In each case, the magic is achieved by the synthesis. In the case of animation, we might say the visual field connects us to the pre-language self, and the voice-over reunites us with our adult self.

The use of animation in therapy is being explored for the first time, and these are preliminary conclusions. However, the clinical evidence for the efficacy of animation is clear. One client, after a lifetime of anxiety, endless medication and a real fear that she could never be free of her 'illness', watched the two-minute 'Octopus' animation and said:

'I realise for the first time my anxiety is not an illness: it's *me*. It's my early self protecting me. And I love the octopus! But – as the video says – maybe my adult me can thank the child and take control.'

Currently we have produced animations on anxiety, depression, trauma, anger and alcohol, and we have upcoming pieces on OCD and avoidance, among others.

Uniting these is the view that common mental health conditions are best seen as adaptive behaviours in response to early nurturing, rather than as illnesses. This is an inherently destigmatising approach.[1]

Finally, since the medium of animation can be viewed privately and anonymously, it may also avoid stigma.

---

1   We call this approach adaptive response theory, or ART. It is in the classic tradition of psychotherapy and, in particular, close to attachment theory, but extends the basic principle to a wider range of presenting problems (for example, to depression).

Real-world therapeutic applications

There are many practical ways animation can help and educate individuals:

1. The most direct is to use the animations in a clinical setting with clients, in one-to-one sessions. They are proving to be a powerful way of reinterpreting a client's lived experience and transforming their cognitive understanding of their mental well-being, thoughts and feelings, symptoms and behaviour.

We have already mentioned the depiction of anxiety as an octopus, our most popular animation to date. In another example, in our award-winning, two-minute animation on anger, we present the idea that anger is not a feeling but rather a soothing strategy learnt in early life. Redefining anger not as a primary emotion but as a choice can – and does – have a transformative effect on a client.

2. We decided to make the animations publicly available for free. This was in response to the mental health crisis that has become more obvious since Covid. We hope and intend that individuals – viewing privately at home – can gain an understanding of their own mental well-being.

3. We intend that these animations can be used in schools, universities and in the corporate environment. Here, student services, HR and well-being departments can use them to engage clients one-to-one or within groups. Discussion can continue after viewing with the use of stills from the animations: 'Which still best represents your main takeaways from the animation?' The animation can then be distributed privately after a session for on-demand viewing.

4. The animations can be used to train staff in student services, HR and well-being departments. This will allow them to better understand the main mental health conditions, and to begin a dialogue with students or employees. While this does not substitute for psychotherapeutic training, it is important that they should have a level of understanding that allows staff working in these areas to signpost those affected to further help.

Indeed, concern for the mental well-being of staff is now not only a legal duty but a basic mark of good management. We can create a culture of self-referral if the process is destigmatising. Being able to view the animations privately, and reinforcing the message that mental heath conditions are less illness than adaptive response, can contribute to the feeling of safety in seeking help.

In universities there is now increasing – and long overdue – focus on the mental welfare of students and, in parallel, a knowledge of increasing legal jeopardy if this is ignored.

5. Finally, we hope that the animations may be useful in public health campaigns; in promoting a general awareness of mental health issues; in aiding self-diagnosis; and in signposting available help, all sitting within an international, national or local scope.

Conclusion

In the past hundred years, animation has become a form of mass entertainment. The exponential rise in computing power means the ability to produce 'broadcast'-quality animation has fallen within the budgets of business. Companies invest in animation because they recognise the benefits as a commutations tool. This trend is only set to continue.

The most recent research in cognitive neuroscience, artificial intelligence, human physiology, philosophy, psychiatry and linguistics have brought us to an exciting intersection. We've acquired greater understanding of human psychology in general and of several presenting problems in particular. Just two exciting takeaways from the latest research are that people actively anticipate and try to predict their environment, then map the world against the stories they carry. Much of this cognitive processing occurs unconsciously.

If dreams were Freud's 'royal road to the unconscious' (1899), it's intriguing to think about the role animation might play in allowing accessibility to parts of the mind that are inaccessible through conscious thought, or as a tool to explain complex dynamics to distressed clients unable to take in novel information via reading.

The route to market has never been more cost effective. Once produced, an animation can be inexpensively spliced and diced to suit multiple audiences within every country, in any format or channel and across every platform. The rise of the internet has meant this distribution is effectively free of charge.

If 'walking with the client' is what therapists do, then animation is a cost-effective additional tool to help therapists walk with them; to help clients explore and creatively explain their lives to themselves.

Here's a real opportunity: the ability of psychotherapy to use animation comes at a time when the NHS (CYPMHS and CAMHS in particular) has never been more financially squeezed. Meanwhile, the education system is experiencing double-digit rise in, for example, self harm by students, and violence towards teachers and TAs. And as mental health provision and education continues in a crisis of chronic underfunding and understaffing, it seems likely the current mental health crisis is set to become endemic.

Now is the time for psychotherapy to continue to 'act locally but think globally', and explore radical new means of intervention on every level: personal, social and universal.

About the Authors

Quint Boa

Quint is Managing Director and Founder of
Shoot You Ltd, an award-winning production company based in London, Amsterdam, New York and Los Angeles.

Quint graduated with an M.A. in Psychotherapy and Counselling from Regents University, and became a UKCP qualified therapist (now retired) with a private practice, specialising in the mind/body relationship and its relationship to addiction.

James Earl

James is a psychotherapist and relationship counsellor in private practice in SW London, with a Masters Degree from the University of Sussex and a Post-Graduate Diploma from Relate. He taught Philosophy for many years at Richmond, The American International University.

James's professional interests include the loss of desire in long-term relationships, rethinking common mental health issues, and the crossover between Philosophy and Psychotherapy.

Acknowledgements

The production of this book would have been impossible without the enthusiastic help of the team at Shoot You. In particular Lucien De Vivo (Senior Creative), Sam Miller (Senior Animator), Becky Hill (Senior Animation Producer), Christopher Harry (Animator). And the irrepressible Billy Wolf (wunderkind).

Printed in Great Britain
by Amazon